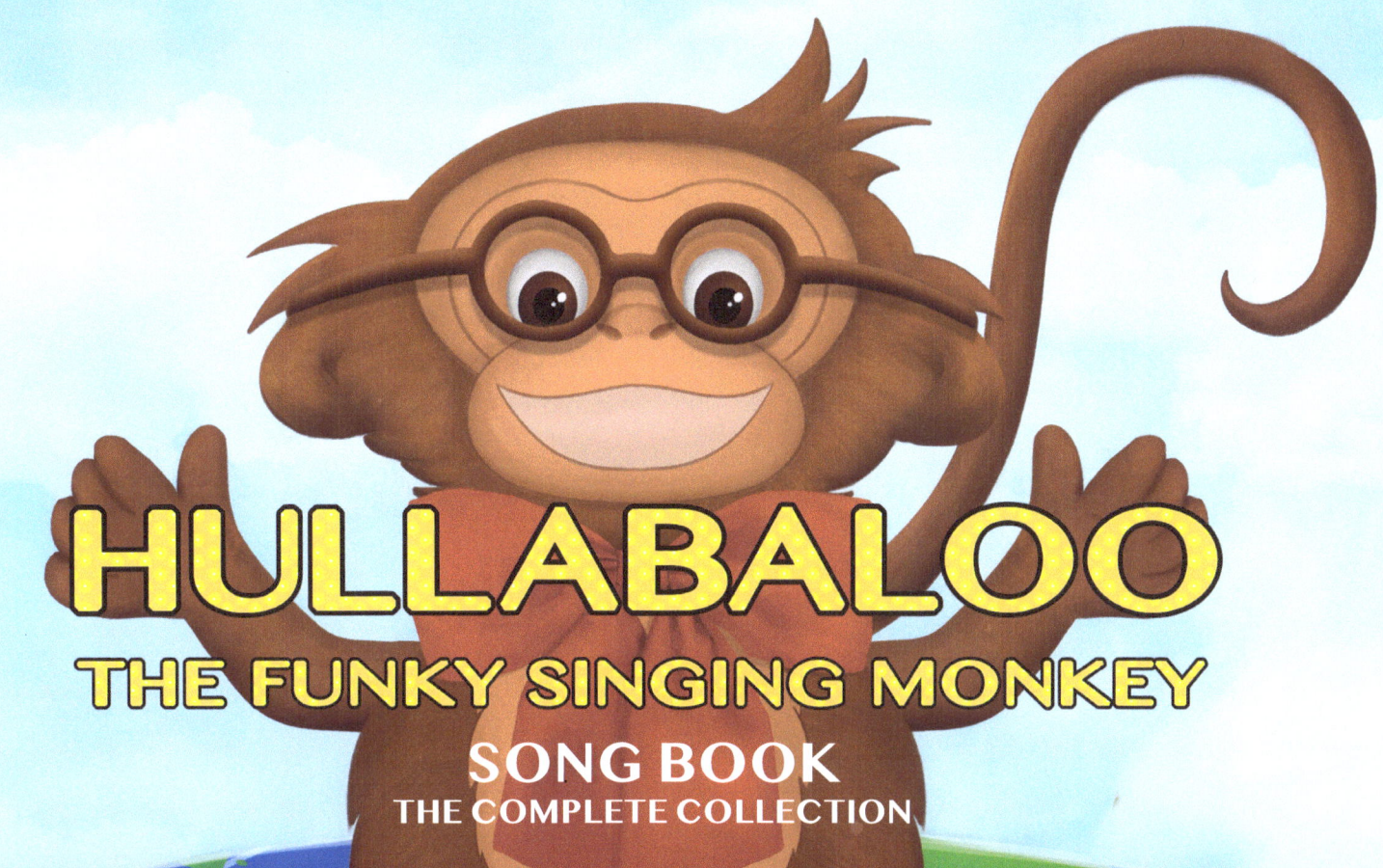

Publishing:
First published by Kindle Direct Publishing, an imprint of Amazon, in 2025

Published by WORLD OF NANCY DAGOSTINO, AUSTRALIA.
ABN: 72 356 082 051
www.worldofnancydagostino.com

Copyright:
For all works contained herein:
Copyright © 2024 Nancy D'Agostino
Copyright ℗ 2024 WORLD OF NANCY DAGOSTINO

All rights reserved. Apart from any use as permitted under the *Copyright Act 1968*, no part may be reproduced without permission. Unauthorised copying, arranging, adapting, recording, internet posting, public performance, or other distribution of the music in this publication is an infringement of copyright. Infringers are liable under law.

info@worldofnancydagostino.com

Moral Rights:
The right of Nancy D'Agostino to be identified as the author, illustrator, composer and recording artist of this work has been asserted by her in accordance with the *Copyright Amendment (Moral Rights) Act 2000*.

A catalogue record for this book is available from the National Library of Australia

Hullabaloo Book Series:
Book 1B: Hullabaloo The Funky Singing Monkey Song Book: The Complete Collection (Supplementary Material) for Hullabaloo The Funky Singing Monkey (Main Book)

ISBN 978-1-7637040-9-1 (8.5 x 11 Paperback)

Publishing Team:
Editor: Nancy D'Agostino
Proof-reading: Nancy D'Agostino & Anne Micallef
Illustrator: Nancy D'Agostino
Publisher: WORLD OF NANCY DAGOSTINO, AUSTRALIA

Book Design:
Stage 1 – Cover Design and Interior Layout by Nancy D'Agostino
Stage 2 – Book Formatting, Revisions and Finished Art by Paul Miller Illustration & Design

Music Team:
Music compositions, voice recordings of scales, songs and voiceover by Singer-Songwriter, Nancy D'Agostino.
Music production & mastering of scales, songs, instrumental tracks, voiceover and sheet music by Music Producer, Peter Bee at Studio Bee.

Artistic Art and Design Process:
Nancy D'Agostino used pencil, ink outlines and COPIC Sketch Markers on paper to create the original artwork, along with a process of traditional tracing paper techniques. This ensured consistency when hand drawing characters, scenery and all elements within the artwork before the original artwork was converted into digital illustrations.

Disclaimer:
This is a work of fiction. Names, characters, places, and incidents are either the product of the author's imagination or used fictitiously. Any resemblance to actual persons, living or dead, events, or locales is purely coincidental. The artwork in this book, features original illustrations. The Broadway scene, features original illustrations inspired by – well known musicals. All signage and imagery have been uniquely created for this book and do not depict actual trademarks. Any resemblance to real musicals is purely coincidental. No endorsement or affiliation with any musical or trademark owner is implied.

Contact:
info@worldofnancydagostino.com

Edition: First Edition 2025

Printed by Amazon KDP and IngramSpark

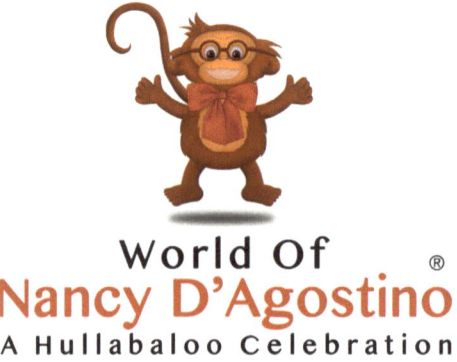

HULLABALOO THE FUNKY SINGING MONKEY SONG BOOK
Music & Lyrics by Nancy D'Agostino

CONTENTS:

Single:
Official Single released, as featured in this Songbook and on iTunes and everywhere.

1. Hullabaloo The Funky Singing Monkey 4
   (2024 Extended Version) ISMN 979-0-9022869-5-4

2019 Original Versions:
As featured in the Children's Book, Audio Book, Colouring Book and Book Trailer.

2. Sing Monkey Scale (5 Up, 4 Down) 6
   ISMN 979-0-9022869-0-9
3. Fiddle Dee Dum (4 Up, 3 Down White Note Scale) 8
   ISMN 979-0-9022869-1-6
4. Lah Arpeggio Scale 10
   ISMN 979-0-9022869-2-3
5. The Aria Song 12
   ISMN 979-0-9022869-3-0
6. Hullabaloo The Funky Singing Monkey 14
   ISMN 979-0-9022869-4-7

2024 Singalong Versions:
As featured on the Album Hullabaloo The Funky Singing Monkey: The Complete Collection.

7. Sing Monkey Scale (5 Up, 4 Down) 16
   (Singalong Version) ISMN 979-0-9022869-6-1
8. Fiddle Dee Dum (4 Up, 3 Down White Note Scale) 18
   (Singalong Version) ISMN 979-0-9022869-7-8
9. Lah Arpeggio Scale 20
   (Singalong Version) ISMN 979-0-9022869-8-5
10. The Aria Song 22
    (Singalong Version) ISMN 979-0-9022869-9-2
11. Hullabaloo The Funky Singing Monkey 25
    (Singalong Version) ISMN 979-0-9022870-4-3

Bonus 2024 Singalong Versions:

12. Sing Hullabaloo Scale (5 Up, 4 Down) 28
    (Singalong Version) ISMN 979-0-9022870-0-5
13. Buzzing Bee Butterfly (4 Up, 3 Down White Note Scale) 30
    (Singalong Version) ISMN 979-0-9022870-1-2
14. Mademoiselle Rose Arpeggio Scale 32
    (Singalong Version) ISMN 979-0-9022870-2-9

Introduction...

Scales can be sung in 2 styles:
1. Legato
2. Staccato

Legato:

Definition: Legato means singing notes in a smooth, connected manner. Each note flows seamlessly into the next without noticeable breaks. Legato begins with a consonant or hum, and then flows smoothly through the vowels.

Technique: In a legato scale, the notes are sung in a smooth, connected manner. Singers often start with a consonant or humming sound (like 'mmm...') before the vowel, but then continue with seamless flow of vowel sounds.

Example: For a 5 Up, 4 Down scale starting on G, you might start with G-A-B-C-D (Ascending) humming into the first note 'Mmm – Ah' and then continue with 'Ah, Ah, Ah, Ah, – and then (Descending) C-B-A-G with Ah, Ah, Ah, Ah.' The initial consonant or hum helps to set the tone, but the focus is on maintaining a continuous, flowing sound.

Purpose: This technique enhances breath control, smoothness and expressiveness. It helps singers develop the ability to sustain notes and create a lyrical melodic line.

Effect: This style creates a lyrical, expressive quality, often used in melodic and emotional passages.

Benefits for Singers:

1. **Improved Tone Quality:** Practicing Legato helps singers develop a rich, full sound, by focusing on smooth, connected notes.
2. **Breath Control:** Legato singing requires continuous breath support, which strengthens the respiratory muscles and improves and enhances overall breath management. This is crucial for sustaining long phrases and maintaining a consistent sound.
3. **Smooth Transitions:** Legato trains singers to move seamlessly between notes, creating a flowing, lyrical sound.
4. **Phrasing and Musicality:** Legato practice helps singers develop a sense of phrasing, allowing for more expressive and emotional performances.
5. **Vocal Agility:** Regular legato practice increases vocal flexibility and control, enabling singers to handle complex melodic lines with ease.

Benefits for Musicians:

1. **Finger Dexterity and Coordination:** For instrumentalists, legato scales improve finger strength and dexterity and coordination, crucial for playing smooth, connected passages.
2. **Hand Coordination:** It improves hand coordination, allowing for more fluid and precise movements across the instrument.
3. **Control over Articulation:** Practicing legato helps musicians develop better control over articulation, leading to a more polished and professional sound.
4. **Musical Expression:** Legato playing adds emotional depth and expressiveness to music, making performances more engaging.
5. **Versatility:** Mastering legato techniques make musicians more versatile, enabling them to perform a wide range of musical styles with greater expressiveness and control.

Staccato:

Definition: Staccato means singing notes in a short, detached manner. Each note is distinct and separated from the others.

Technique: In a staccato scale, each note is sung in a short, detached manner. To achieve this effect, singers often use a consonant before each vowel sound. This helps to clearly articulate each note and create the desired separation.

Example: For a 5 Up, 4 Down scale starting on G, you might sing G-A-B-C-D (Ascending) 'Noh, Noh, Noh, Noh, Noh, – and then (Descending) C-B-A-G with Noh, Noh, Noh, Noh.' The consonants here provide a crisp attack for each note, enhancing the staccato effect.

Purpose: This technique helps improve precision, articulation, and rhythmic accuracy. It also trains the singer to control breath and maintain clarity in fast passages.

Effect: This style adds rhythm and energy to the music, making it lively and dynamic.

Benefits for Singers:

1. **Improved Articulation:** Staccato scales help singers develop precise articulation making each note clear and distinct.
2. **Breath Control:** Practicing staccato requires quick, controlled breaths, which strengthens the respiratory system and enhances overall breath management.
3. **Rhythmic Precision:** Staccato singing improves a singer's sense of timing and rhythm, essential for performing fast-paced and rhythmically complex pieces.
4. **Dynamic Contrast:** It adds variety and texture to vocal performances, allowing singers to create dynamic emphasis with certain notes or phrases.
5. **Vocal Agility:** Regular practice of staccato scales increases vocal agility, enabling singers to navigate rapid note changes with ease.

Benefits for Musicians:

1. **Finger Dexterity:** For instrumentalists, staccato scales enhance finger strength and dexterity, crucial for playing fast and intricate passages.
2. **Precision and Control:** Staccato practice improves note accuracy and control, leading to cleaner and more precise playing.
3. **Rhythmic Accuracy:** It helps musicians develop a strong sense of rhythm and timing, which is vital for ensemble playing and solo performance.
4. **Expressiveness:** Staccato adds an expressive element to music, allowing musicians to highlight rhythms and create a lively, energetic sound.
5. **Versatility:** Mastering staccato techniques make musicians more versatile, enabling them to perform a wide range of musical styles with greater expressiveness and control.

By practicing both legato and staccato styles, singers and musicians can develop a versatile vocal technique that allows them to perform a wide range of musical pieces with precision and expressiveness.

Hullabaloo was one in a million – Rocking this town like Annie on Broadway.

– Nancy D'Agostino

Instructions:

**Hullabaloo The Funky Singing Monkey
(2024 Extended Version)**
– New song written exclusively for the Song Book and Official Single release, also featured on the compilation albums.

The Official Single Release:

Vocal Training:
This catchy and vibrant rhyme song is the 'Official main Single Release' for the Children's Picture Book 'Hullabaloo The Funky Singing Monkey' available on iTunes and everywhere. With its jazz inspired vibe and catchy, playful, descriptive, rhyming lyrics… it's a real showstopper. Written, Composed and Performed by Nancy D'Agostino, this sing-along version will have you singing solo in not time.

Purpose: The sing-along theme encourages interactive participation and group participation making it a fun and engaging activity whilst building confidence to where you can also sing solo or with others over the instrumental music. Singing along will also help improve your pitch, accuracy, timing and vocal control, and musicality. Add some dance moves or basic movement, hand gestures and facial expression as you explore the fun and excitement of performing and acting out this song all about Hullabaloo!

Piano Training:
Playing this extended version helps musicians develop finger dexterity and hand coordination as you play the melody, chords and instrumental sections. It will also enhance your understanding of rhythm and timing, as you will need to synchronize your playing with the music. Additionally, practicing this piece improves sight-reading skills and musical interpretation, as you learn to follow the sheet music and express the song's jazzy vibe.

Purpose: This engaging fun piece offers several benefits for young musicians. This sing-along version will help with finger dexterity and hand coordination and encourages consistent practice and builds confidence in your piano abilities.

HULLABALOO THE FUNKY SINGING MONKEY
(2024 EXTENDED VERSION)

Words and Music by NANCY D'AGOSTINO
Arranged by PETER BEE
Performed by NANCY D'AGOSTINO

Introduction:
Ladies and gentlemen, boys and girls, singalong to the song!

ISMN 979-0-9022869-5-4

Copyright © 2024 Nancy DAgostino

ISRC
TCAJD2458970

ORIGINALS
The original 2019 versions as featured in the Children's Picture Book, e-Book and Audio Book.

Singing Scales and Songs is easier than you think. All you have to do is sing in tune and sing-along!

– Nancy D'Agostino

Instructions:

Sing Monkey Scale (5 Up, 4 Down)

Vocal Training: 🎤
Staccato: When singing the 5 Up, 4 Down Scale (commonly known as the 'five-tone scale' or 'five-note scale') for example, ascending G-A-B-C-D and descending C–B-A-G in staccato, each note should be short and detached. Focus on clear articulation and breath support to maintain steady pitch and control before starting each scale run. Sing and act out this scale in staccato style on one breath, as is common practice with contemporary singing and voice acting to add a lively, energetic and playful character to the music just like Hullabaloo.

Purpose: This vocal technique helps the singer and voice actors to improve precision, articulation, and rhythmic accuracy. It also challenges them to control their breath and maintain clarity in fast passages as part of a vocal warm-up and deliver the scale in the voice of the character.

Piano Training: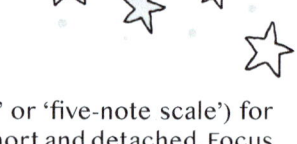
Start by playing the 5 Up, 4 Down Scale (commonly known as the 'five-tone scale' or 'five-note scale') for example, ascending G-A-B-C-D and descending C–B-A-G with one finger per note, using the right hand. Play each note in staccato style, making each note short and detached.

Purpose: Practicing the 5 Up, 4 Down Scale on the piano can help you develop basic piano skills. This exercise will help you to improve finger strength, dexterity, and coordination. Additionally, it reinforces the concept of musical scales and enhances your understanding of pitch and rhythm. As you become more comfortable you can try playing the scale with both hands.

SING MONKEY SCALE (5 UP, 4 DOWN)

Words and Music by NANCY D'AGOSTINO
Arranged by PETER BEE
Performed by NANCY D'AGOSTINO (as the voice of Hullabaloo)

Oo oo oo ah ah oo oo ah ah

Copyright © 2018 Nancy D'Agostino

Twiddle your thumbs and sing the Fiddle Dee Dum…

– Nancy D'Agostino

Instructions:

Fiddle Dee Dum (4 Up, 3 Down White Note Scale)

Vocal Training:
Scale Song: When singing the 4 Up, 3 Down White Note Scale, (essentially a sequence of four-note groups on white keys on the piano) a creative scale developed by Nancy D'Agostino specifically for Vocal Training with a Jazz influence that will help with improvisation. For example, starting on G3 (G below Middle C) sing ascending G-A-B-C and descending B-A-G. Then move up to A and sing ascending A-B-C-D and descending C-B-A. Then move back down to G and sing ascending G-A-B-C and descending B-A-G. Sing each scale on a separate breath ascending and descending making sure to sing the words with clarity for good pronunciation and remember to stay in character and sing just like Hullabaloo.

Purpose: This exercise helps singers with Pitch Recognition, in helping them to hear and recognize sharps and flats as is often included in more complex music. This scale pattern is an excellent warm up for singing and voice acting.

Piano Training:
Essentially a sequence of ascending and descending tetra chords (four-note groups) on white keys of the piano. This pattern doesn't correspond to a specific traditional scale in classical music theory but can be understood as a series of diatonic tetra chords. For example, starting on G3 (G below Middle C) ascending G-A-B-C and descending B-A-G. Then moving up to A and ascending A-B-C-D and descending C-B-A. Then moving back down to the starting note G and ascending G-A-B-C and descending B-A-G.

Purpose: This exercise is excellent for developing finger strength, dexterity, ear training and familiarity with the keyboard as well as great for warm-up exercises.

FIDDLE DEE DUM (4 UP, 3 DOWN WHITE NOTE SCALE)

Words and Music by NANCY D'AGOSTINO
Arranged by PETER BEE
Performed by NANCY D'AGOSTINO (as the voice of Hullabaloo)

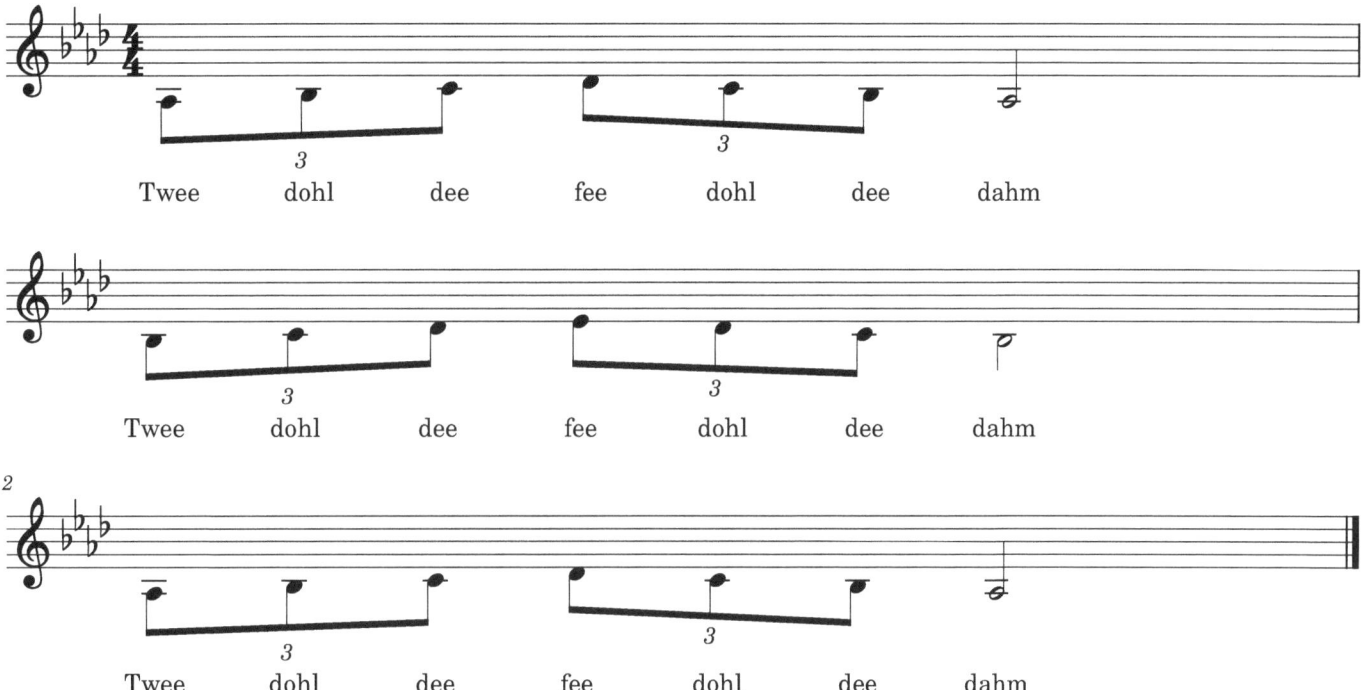

Copyright © 2018 Nancy D'Agostino

Now the show must go on – so if you can sing, sing-along.

– Nancy D'Agostino

Instructions:
Lah Arpeggio Scale

Vocal Training:
When singing the arpeggio scale you are typically singing the notes of a chord that can span multiple octaves and be sung in ascending and descending, or in both directions. Sing each scale on a separate breath to support your voice through the note changes and maintain vocal release. Aim to keep your mouth agile without tension as you sing the scale with good pronunciation in the character of the leading lady, Mademoiselle Rose just like a seasoned pro!

Purpose: Singing arpeggios helps with ear training to improve your pitch recognition and to reproduce intervals and helps singers to expand and control their vocal range. Repeated practice helps singers with muscle memory helping to navigate between notes smoothly and hit notes accurately when making larger leaps between pitches and is great as part of a vocal warm-up.

Piano Training:
An arpeggio is commonly known as a broken chord, and is sometimes referred to as rolled chord where the notes of a chord are played in succession, rather than simultaneously. For example a G major arpeggio would include the notes G-B-D. When played in sequence, it might look like G-B-D-G ascending and then G-D-B-G descending.

Purpose: Playing arpeggios on the piano will help with finger dexterity and strength, and improve hand coordination smoothly across the keyboard, concentration and focus, emotional expression, confidence and self-esteem. With regular practice, arpeggios will help you to improve your overall technical skills and musical understanding.

LAH ARPEGGIO SCALE

Words and Music by NANCY D'AGOSTINO
Arranged by PETER BEE
Performed by NANCY D'AGOSTINO (as the voice of the Leading Lady)

Lah lah lah lah lah lah lah   Lah lah lah lah lah lah lah   Lah lah lah lah lah lah lah

ISMN 979-0-9022869-2-3

Copyright © 2018 Nancy D'Agostino

ISRC

Then when Mademoiselle Rose sang 'The Aria Song', Hullabaloo sang it too.

– Nancy D'Agostino

Instructions:
The Aria Song

Vocal Training:
An aria is a solo vocal piece, typically found in operas, where an orchestra accompanies the singer. The word 'aria' comes from the Italian word 'air' and was originally referred to as an expressive elaborate melody. This aria song is designed to showcase your vocal skills and emotional expression as you sing in the character of the leading lady 'Mademoiselle Rose.

Purpose: Singing arias helps to develop advanced vocal techniques, including breath control, articulation, and dynamic range, emotional expression, muscle memory to perform challenging pieces, versatility with a mix of legato (smooth) and staccato (short, detached) notes, as well as sustained notes. This aria is a little tricky where you get to sing and act out Mademoiselle Rose and Hullabaloo character parts.

Piano Training:
Practicing the aria over and over is essential when playing intricate aria melodies that require good coordination, where you may need to play different rhythms and dynamics with each hand. Playing the aria will allow you to connect emotionally with the music, and help you build confidence in becoming an expressive pianist.

Purpose: Playing arias on a piano helps develop finger strength and dexterity, hand coordination, and musical understanding of musical structure, harmony and phrasing that are essential for interpreting and performing music.

THE ARIA SONG

Words and Music by NANCY D'AGOSTINO
Arranged by PETER BEE
Performed by NANCY D'AGOSTINO (as the voices of Hullabaloo and the Leading Lady)

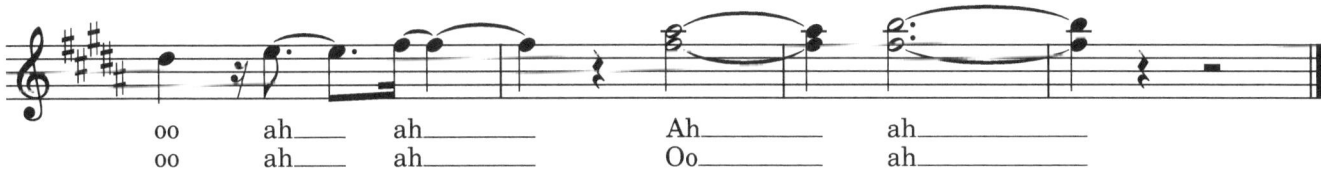

ISMN 979-0-9022869-3-0

Copyright © 2018 Nancy D'Agostino

ISRC
TCAEU2087027

Maybe someday he'll have his name up in lights and his name will be famous!

– Nancy D'Agostino

Instructions:

Hullabaloo The Funky Singing Monkey

Vocal Training:
This is the 2019 Original Version of the rhyme song for 'Hullabaloo The Funky Singing Monkey' Children's Picture Book (also featured in the Audio book, Colouring Book and Book Trailer). Written, Composed and Performed by Nancy D'Agostino, this rhyme song is short and sweet and a little tricky, as you will have to learn the words that tell the story in reverse. Follow along and have fun singing along with the Notated Sheet Music.

Purpose: It's designed to be sung and or played on piano and would be a great performance song by adding some dance moves or basic movement, hand gestures and facial expressions and where you can make your stage debut just like Hullabaloo.

Whether you're a vocalist or a pianist, this song is sure to bring joy and energy to your repertoire.

Piano Training:
Playing this sing-along version helps musicians develop finger dexterity and hand coordination as you play the melody, chords and instrumental sections. It will also enhance your understanding of rhythm and timing, as you will need to synchronize your playing with the music. Additionally, practicing this piece improves sight-reading skills and musical interpretation, as you learn to follow the sheet music and express the song's jazzy vibe.

Purpose: This engaging fun piece offers several benefits for young musicians. This sing-along version will help with finger dexterity and hand coordination and encourages consistent practice and builds confidence in your piano abilities.

'Life's a celebration!' – Nancy D'Agostino

HULLABALOO THE FUNKY SINGING MONKEY

Words and Music by NANCY D'AGOSTINO
Arranged by PETER BEE
Performed by NANCY D'AGOSTINO

Introduction:
Ladies and gentlemen, boys and girls, singalong to the song!

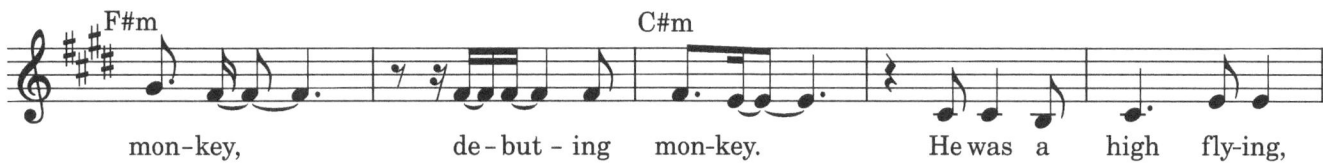

ISMN 979-0-9022869-4-7

Copyright © 2018 Nancy D'Agostino

ISRC

SING-ALONGS

These special 2024 sing-along versions take the original 2019 versions and extends them with additional instrumental music so that you can sing-along and hone your vocal skills.

Singing Scales and Songs is easier than you think. All you have to do is sing in tune and sing-along!

– Nancy D'Agostino

Instructions:

Sing Monkey Scale (5 Up, 4 Down) (Singalong Version)

Vocal Training:
Staccato: When singing the 5 Up, 4 Down Scale [Singalong Version] (commonly known as the 'five-tone scale' or 'five-note scale') for example, ascending G-A-B-C-D and descending C–B–A-G in staccato, each note should be short and detached. Focus on clear articulation and breath support to maintain steady pitch and control before starting each scale run. Sing each scale in staccato style on one breath, as is common practice with contemporary singing to add a lively, energetic and playful character to the music just like Hullabaloo.

Purpose: This vocal technique helps the singer to improve precision, articulation, and rhythmic accuracy. It also challenges the singer to control breath and maintain clarity in fast passages as part of a vocal warm-up.

Piano Training:
Start by playing the 5 Up, 4 Down Scale [Singalong Version] (commonly known as the 'five-tone scale' or 'five note scale') for example, ascending G-A-B-C-D and descending C–B-A-G with one finger per note, using the right hand. Play each note in staccato style, making each note short and detached.

Purpose: Practicing the 5 Up, 4 Down Scale on the piano can help you develop basic piano skills. This exercise will help you to improve finger strength, dexterity, and coordination. Additionally, it reinforces the concept of musical scales and enhances your understanding of pitch and rhythm. As you become more comfortable you can try playing the scale with both hands.

SING MONKEY SCALE (5 UP, 4 DOWN)
(SINGALONG VERSION)

Words and Music by NANCY D'AGOSTINO
Arranged by PETER BEE
Performed by NANCY D'AGOSTINO (as the voice of Hullabaloo)

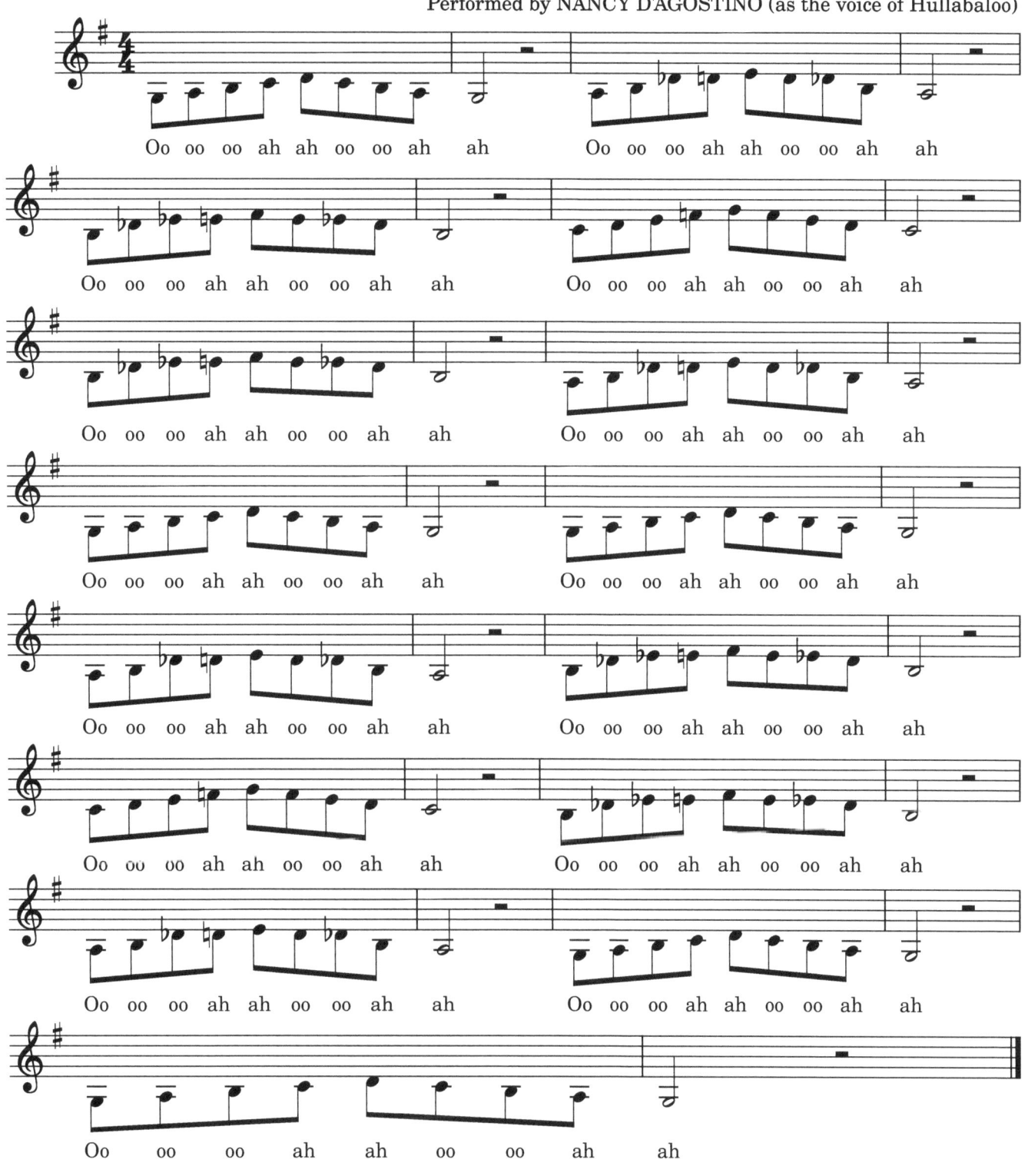

Copyright © 2024 Nancy DAgostino

Twiddle your thumbs and sing the Fiddle Dee Dum…

– Nancy D'Agostino

Instructions:

Fiddle Dee Dum (4 Up, 3 Down White Note Scale)
(Singalong Version)

Vocal Training:
Scale Song: When singing the 4 Up, 3 Down White Note Scale, (essentially a sequence of four-note groups on white keys of the piano) a creative scale developed by Nancy D'Agostino specifically for Vocal Training with a Jazz influence that will help with improvisation. For example, starting on G3 (G below Middle C) sing ascending G-A-B-C and descending B-A-G. Then move up to A and sing ascending A-B-C-D and descending C-B-A. Then move back down to G and sing ascending G-A-B-C and descending B-A-G. Sing each scale on a separate breath ascending and descending making sure to sing the words with clarity for good pronunciation and remember to be expressive just like Hullabaloo.

Purpose: This exercise helps singers with Pitch Recognition, in helping them to hear and recognize sharps and flats as is often included in more complex music. This will help you gain a strong sense of pitch within the diatonic scale. This scale pattern is an excellent warm up.

Piano Training:
Essentially a sequence of ascending and descending tetra chords (four-note groups) on white keys of the piano. This pattern doesn't correspond to a specific traditional scale in classical music theory but can be understood as a series of diatonic tetra chords. For example, starting on G3 (G below Middle C) ascending G-A-B-C and descending B-A-G. Then moving up to A and ascending A-B-C-D and descend C-B-A. Then moving back down to the starting note G and ascending G-A-B-C and descending B-A-G.

Purpose: This exercise is excellent for developing finger strength, dexterity, ear training and familiarity with the keyboard as well as great for warm-up exercises.

FIDDLE DEE DUM (4 UP, 3 DOWN WHITE NOTE SCALE)
(SINGALONG VERSION)

Words and Music by NANCY D'AGOSTINO
Arranged by PETER BEE
Performed by NANCY D'AGOSTINO (as the voice of Hullabaloo)

Copyright © 2024 Nancy D'Agostino

Now the show must go on – so if you can sing, sing-along.

– Nancy D'Agostino

Instructions:

Lah Arpeggio Scale (Singalong Version)

Vocal Training:
When singing the arpeggio scale you are typically singing the notes of a chord that can span multiple octaves and be sung in ascending and descending, or in both directions. Sing each scale on a separate breath to support your voice through the note changes and maintain vocal release. Aim to keep your mouth agile without tension as you sing the scale song with good pronunciation.

Purpose: Singing arpeggios helps with ear training to improve your pitch recognition and to reproduce intervals and helps singers to expand and control their vocal range. Repeated practice helps singers with muscle memory helping to navigate between notes smoothly and hit notes accurately when making larger leaps between pitches and is great as part of a vocal warm-up.

Piano Training:
An arpeggio is commonly known as a broken chord, and is sometimes referred to as rolled chord where the notes of a chord are played in succession, rather than simultaneously. For example a G major arpeggio would include the notes G-B-D. When played in sequence, it might look like G-B-D-G ascending and then G-D-B-G descending.

Purpose: Playing arpeggios on the piano will help with finger dexterity and strength, and improve hand coordination smoothly across the keyboard, concentration and focus, emotional expression, confidence and self-esteem. With regular practice, arpeggios will help you to improve your overall technical skills and musical understanding.

LAH ARPEGGIO SCALE
(SINGALONG VERSION)

Words and Music by NANCY D'AGOSTINO
Arranged by PETER BEE
Performed by NANCY D'AGOSTINO (as the voice of the Leading Lady)

Copyright © 2024 Nancy D'Agostino

Then when Mademoiselle Rose sang 'The Aria Song', Hullabaloo sang it too.

– Nancy D'Agostino

Instructions:

**The Aria Song
(Singalong Version)**

Vocal Training:
An aria is a solo vocal piece, typically found in operas, where an orchestra accompanies the singer. The word 'aria' comes from the Italian word 'air' and was originally referred to an expressive elaborate melody. This aria song is designed to showcase your vocal skills and emotional expression as you sing in the character of the leading lady 'Mademoiselle Rose'. Sing the notes with precision and aim to 'paint the town cherry red' and earn a standing ovation when you hit the big note at the end of the aria.

Purpose: Singing arias helps to develop advanced vocal techniques, including breath control, articulation, and dynamic range, emotional expression, muscle memory to perform challenging pieces, versatility with a mix of legato (smooth) and staccato (short, detached) notes, as well as sustained notes.

Piano Training:
Practicing the aria over and over is essential when playing intricate aria melodies that require good coordination, where you may need to play different rhythms and dynamics with each hand. Playing the aria will allow you to connect emotionally with the music, and help you build confidence in becoming an expressive pianist.

Purpose: Playing arias on a piano helps develop finger strength and dexterity, hand coordination, and musical understanding of musical structure, harmony and phrasing that are essential for interpreting and performing music.

THE ARIA SONG
(SINGALONG VERSION)

Words and Music by NANCY D'AGOSTINO
Arranged by PETER BEE
Performed by NANCY D'AGOSTINO (as the voices of Hullabaloo and the Leading Lady)

Copyright © 2024 Nancy D'Agostino

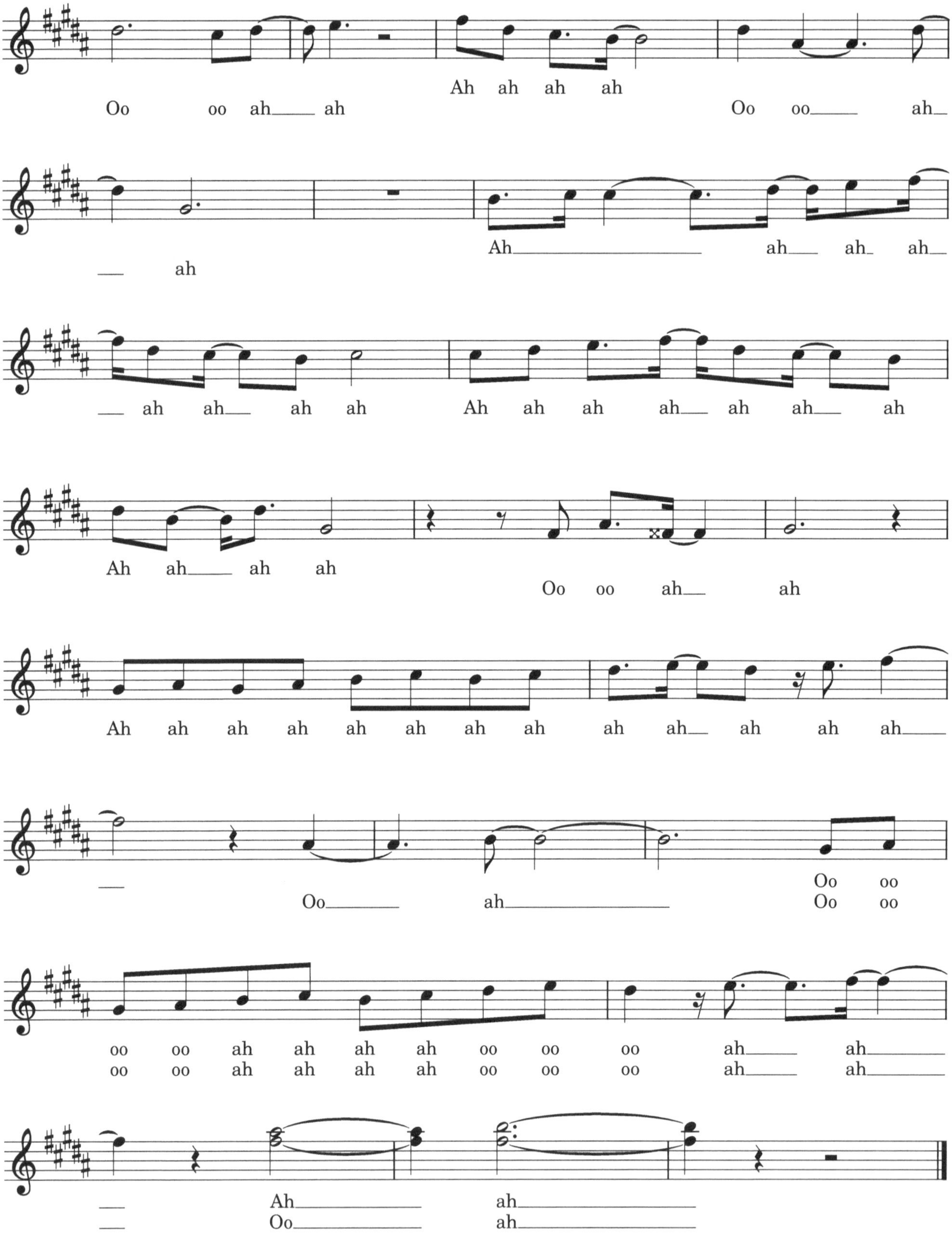

Maybe someday he'll have his name up in lights and his name will be famous!

– Nancy D'Agostino

Instructions:

**Hullabaloo The Funky Singing Monkey
(Singalong Version)**

Vocal Training:
This special sing-along version of 'Hullabaloo The Funky Singing Monkey' takes the 2019 Original Version of the rhyme song and extends it with additional instrumental music (as featured in the Children's Picture Book, Audio Book, Colouring Book and Book Trailer) and is perfect to sing-along with and then seamlessly transitions into an instrumental music section where you get to be the star of the show and sing your solo! You may even want to sing along with family and friends or sing it at school in a supportive environment such as a classroom setting with your teacher and maybe put on a group performance for Book Week (Children's Book Council of Australia) or others held around the world. Nancy D'Agostino performs this catchy jazz inspired rhyme song. It's double short and sweet and a little tricky, as you will have to learn the words that tell the story in reverse.

Purpose: The sing-along theme encourages interactive participation and group participation making it a fun and engaging activity whilst building confidence to where you can also sing solo or with others over the instrumental music. Singing along will also help improve your pitch, accuracy, timing, vocal control and musicality. Add some movement and hand gestures and even some facial expressions as you explore the fun and excitement of performing and acting out this theme song.

Piano Training:
Playing this sing-along version helps musicians develop finger dexterity and hand coordination as you play the melody, chords and instrumental sections. It will also enhance your understanding of rhythm and timing, as you will need to synchronize your playing with the music. Additionally, practicing this piece improves sight-reading skills and musical interpretation, as you learn to follow the sheet music and express the song's jazzy vibe.

Purpose: This engaging fun piece offers several benefits for young musicians. This sing-along version will help with finger dexterity and hand coordination and encourages consistent practice and builds confidence in your piano abilities.

HULLABALOO THE FUNKY SINGING MONKEY
(SINGALONG VERSION)

Words and Music by NANCY D'AGOSTINO
Arranged by PETER BEE
Performed by NANCY D'AGOSTINO

Introduction:
Ladies and gentlemen, boys and girls, singalong to the song!

He was a slam dunk-it' sup - er star spun -

- ky, show stopp - ing mon - key, de - but - ing

mon - key. He was a high fly - ing, twi - ddl - y fi - ddl - y,

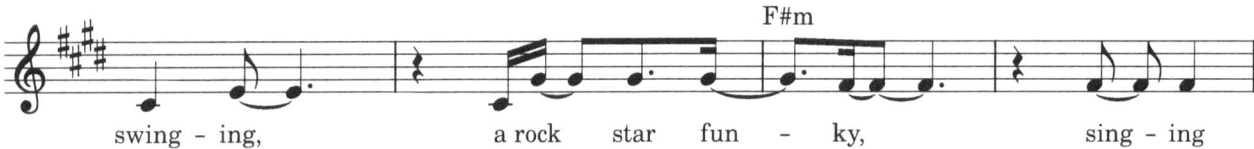
swing - ing, a rock star fun - ky, sing - ing

mon - key. And his name was Hull - a - ba -

loo from Tim - buk - tu — **Hull - a - ba - loo!** **The fun -**

- ky sing - ing mo - / - - / - nkey!

ISMN 979-0-9022870-4-3

Copyright © 2024 Nancy D'Agostino

ISRC

TCAJC2411682

Copyright © 2024 Nancy D'Agostino

27

BONUS SING-ALONGS

All you have to do is sing, sing in tune and sing along! Said Hullabaloo.

– Nancy D'Agostino

Instructions:

Sing Hullabaloo Scale (5 Up, 4 Down) (Singalong Version)

Vocal Training:
When singing the 5 Up, 4 Down Scale (commonly known as the 'five-tone scale' or 'five-note scale') for example, ascending G-A-B-C-D and descending C-B-A-G. Focus on clear articulation and breath support to maintain steady pitch and control before starting each scale run. Sing each scale song on one breath with good pronunciation, to add a lively, energetic and playful feel to the name of the character 'Hullabaloo!'

Purpose: This vocal technique helps the singer to improve precision, articulation, and rhythmic accuracy. It also challenges the singer to control breath and maintain clarity in fast passages as part of a vocal warm-up.

Piano Training:
Start by playing the 5 Up, 4 Down Scale (commonly known as the 'five-tone scale' or 'five-note scale') for example, ascending G-A-B-C-D and descending C–B-A-G with one finger per note, using the right hand. Play each note in staccato style, making each note short and detached.

Purpose: Practicing the 5 Up, 4 Down Scale on the piano can help you develop basic piano skills. This exercise will help you to improve finger strength, dexterity, and coordination. Additionally, it reinforces the concept of musical scales and enhances your understanding of pitch and rhythm. As you become more comfortable you can try playing the scale with both hands.

SING HULLABALOO SCALE (5 UP, 4 DOWN)
(SINGALONG VERSION)

Words and Music by NANCY D'AGOSTINO
Arranged by PETER BEE
Performed by NANCY D'AGOSTINO (as the voice of Hullabaloo)

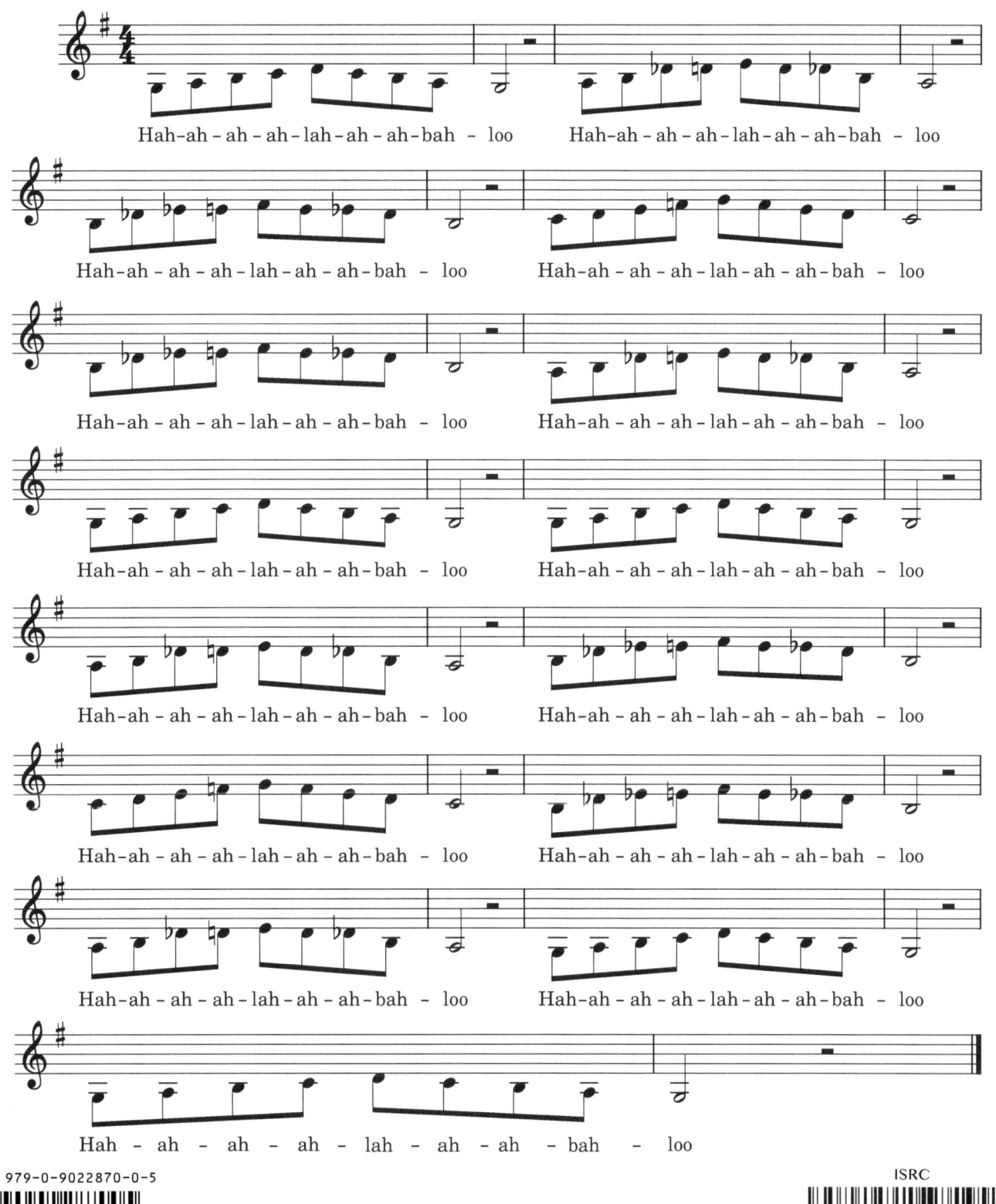

ISMN 979-0-9022870-0-5

Copyright © 2024 Nancy D'Agostino

Then with the breeze came the butterflies and a buzzing bee. Bzzzz…

– Nancy D'Agostino

Instructions:

Buzzing Bee Butterfly (4 Up, 3 Down White Note Scale)
(Singalong Version)

Vocal Training:
Scale Song: When singing the 4 Up, 3 Down White Note Scale, (essentially a sequence of four-note groups on white keys of the piano) a creative scale developed by Nancy D'Agostino specifically for Vocal Training with a Jazz influence that will help with improvisation. For example, starting on G3 (G below Middle C) sing ascending G-A-B-C and descending B-A-G. Then move up to A and sing ascending A-B-C-D and descending C-B-A. Then move back down to G and sing ascending G-A-B-C and descending B-A-G. Sing each scale on a separate breath ascending and descending making sure to sing the words with clarity for good pronunciation and remember to be expressive just like the leading lady, Mademoiselle Rose.

Purpose: This exercise helps singers with Pitch Recognition, in helping them to hear and recognize sharps and flats as is often included in more complex music. This will help you gain a strong sense of pitch within the diatonic scale. This scale pattern is an excellent warm up.

Piano Training:
Essentially a sequence of ascending and descending tetra chords (four-note groups) on white keys of the piano. This pattern doesn't correspond to a specific traditional scale in classical music theory but can be understood as a series of diatonic tetra chords. For example, starting on G3 (G below Middle C) ascending G-A-B-C and descending B-A-G. Then moving up to A and ascending A-B-C-D and descending C-B-A. Then moving back down to the starting note G and ascending G-A-B-C and descending B-A-G.

Purpose: This exercise is excellent for developing finger strength, dexterity, ear training and familiarity with the keyboard as well as great for warm-up exercises.

BUZZING BEE BUTTERFLY (4 UP, 3 DOWN WHITE NOTE SCALE)
(SINGALONG VERSION)

Words and Music by NANCY D'AGOSTINO
Arranged by PETER BEE
Performed by NANCY D'AGOSTINO (as the voice of Hullabaloo)

ISMN 979-0-9022870-1-2

Copyright © 2024 Nancy D'Agostino

ISRC

31

She sang the arpeggio up and down and it seemed like nothing could stop her now!

– Nancy D'Agostino

Instructions:

Mademoiselle Rose Arpeggio Scale (Singalong Version)

Vocal Training:
When singing the arpeggio scale you are typically singing the notes of a chord that can span multiple octaves and be sung in ascending and descending, or in both directions. Sing each scale on a separate breath to support your voice through the note changes and maintain vocal release. Aim to keep your mouth agile without tension as you sing the scale song with good pronunciation.

Purpose: Singing arpeggios helps with ear training to improve your pitch recognition and to reproduce intervals and helps singers to expand and control their vocal range. Repeated practice helps singers with muscle memory helping to navigate between notes smoothly and hit notes accurately when making larger leaps between pitches and is great as part of a vocal warm-up.

Piano Training:
An arpeggio is commonly known as a broken chord, and is sometimes referred to as rolled chord where the notes of a chord are played in succession, rather than simultaneously. For example a G major arpeggio would include the notes G-B-D. When played in sequence, it might look like G-B-D-G ascending and then G-D-B-G descending.

Purpose: Playing arpeggios on the piano will help with finger dexterity and strength, and improve hand coordination smoothly across the keyboard, concentration and focus, emotional expression, confidence and self-esteem. With regular practice, arpeggios will help you to improve your overall technical skills and musical understanding.

MADEMOISELLE ROSE ARPEGGIO SCALE
(SINGALONG VERSION)

Words and Music by NANCY D'AGOSTINO
Arranged by PETER BEE
Performed by NANCY D'AGOSTINO (as the voice of the Leading Lady)

ISMN 979-0-9022870-2-9

Copyright © 2024 Nancy D'Agostino

ISRC
TCAJB2412059

CHILDREN'S PICTURE BOOK

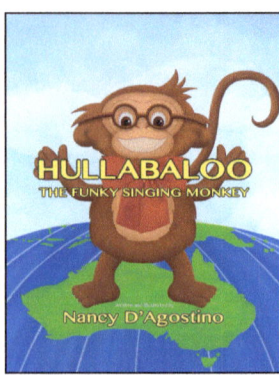

Hullabaloo The Funky Singing Monkey

8" x 10" Paperback
ISBN 978-1-7637040-0-8

8.5" x 11" Paperback
ISBN 978-1-7637040-8-4

8.5" x 11" Hardcover
ISBN 978-1-7637040-3-9

8.5" x 11" E-Book
ISBN 978-1-7637040-2-2

AUDIO BOOK

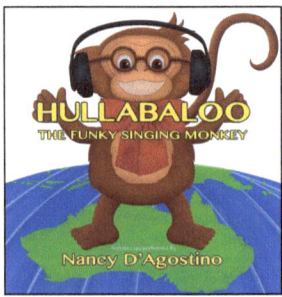

Hullabaloo The Funky Singing Monkey
ISBN 978-1-7637040-7-7
ISRC AU-Q6L-24-00001

MUSIC SOUND RECORDING

Single:
– 2019 Original Version as featured in the Children's Picture Book, Audio Book, Colouring Book and Book Trailer

Hullabaloo The Funky Singing Monkey
ISRC: TCAJB2411737

COLOURING BOOK

Hullabaloo The Funky Singing Monkey Colouring Book

8.5" x 11" Paperback
ISBN 978-1-7637040-4-6

Hullabaloo: The Complete Colouring Book Collection

8.5" x 11" Paperback
ISBN 978-1-7637916-8-8

SONG BOOK

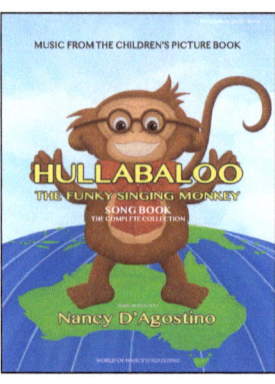

Hullabaloo The Funky Singing Monkey Song Book: The Complete Collection

8.5" x 11" Paperback
ISBN 978-1-7637040-9-1

8.5" x 11" Hardcover
ISBN 978-1-7637916-0-2

8.5" x 11" E-Book
ISBN 978-1-7637916-1-9

Contents:

Single:
– Official Single released, as featured in this Songbook and on iTunes and everywhere:

1. Hullabaloo The Funky Singing Monkey (2024 Extended Version)
   ISMN 979-0-9022869-5-4

2019 Original Versions:
– as featured in the Children's Book, Audio Book, Colouring Book and Book Trailer:

2. Sing Monkey Scale (5 Up, 4 Down)
   ISMN 979-0-9022869-0-9
3. Fiddle Dee Dum (4 Up, 3 Down White Note Scale)
   ISMN 979-0-9022869-1-6
4. Lah Arpeggio Scale
   ISMN 979-0-9022869-2-3
5. The Aria Song
   ISMN 979-0-9022869-3-0
6. Hullabaloo The Funky Singing Monkey
   ISMN 979-0-9022869-4-7

2024 Singalong Versions:

7. Sing Monkey Scale (5 Up, 4 Down) (Singalong Version)
   ISMN 979-0-9022869-6-1
8. Fiddle Dee Dum (4 Up, 3 Down White Note Scale) (Singalong Version)
   ISMN 979-0-9022869-7-8
9. Lah Arpeggio Scale (Singalong Version)
   ISMN 979-0-9022869-8-5
10. The Aria Song (Singalong Version)
    ISMN 979-0-9022869-9-2
11. Hullabaloo The Funky Singing Monkey (Singalong Version)
    ISMN 979-0-9022870-4-3

Bonus 2024 Singalong Versions:

12. Sing Hullabaloo Scale (5 Up, 4 Down) (Singalong Version)
    ISMN 979-0-9022870-0-5
13. Buzzing Bee Butterfly (4 Up, 3 Down White Note Scale) (Singalong Version)
    ISMN 979-0-9022870-1-2
14. Mademoiselle Rose Arpeggio Scale (Singalong Version)
    ISMN 979-0-9022870-2-9

MUSIC VIDEO RECORDINGS

Book Trailer:
Hullabaloo The Funky Singing Monkey
ISBN 978-1-7637040-0-8
ISRC: TCAJB2411737

Music Video – Single:
Hullabaloo The Funky Singing Monkey
(2024 Extended Version)
ISBN 978-1-7637040-0-8
ISRC: TCAJD2458970

MUSIC SOUND RECORDINGS

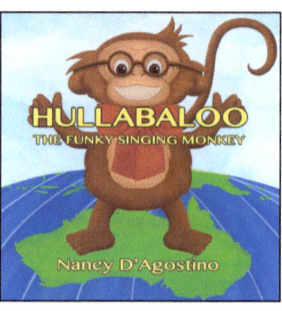

Single:

Hullabaloo The Funky Singing Monkey (2024 Extended Version)
– Official Single Released – as featured in the Songbook, on iTunes and everywhere
ISRC TCAJD2458970   UPC: 859799231290

Albums:

Hullabaloo The Funky Singing Monkey: The Complete Collection
UPC 859798417596

1. Hullabaloo The Funky Singing Monkey (2024 Extended Version)
   ISRC: TCAJD2458970
2. Sing Monkey Scale
   ISRC: TCAEU2086945
3. Fiddle Dee Dum
   ISRC: TCAEU2086959
4. Lah Arpeggio Scale
   ISRC: TCAEU2086973
5. The Aria Song
   ISRC: TCAEU2087027
6. Hullabaloo The Funky Singing Monkey
   ISRC: TCAJB2411737
7. Sing Monkey Scale (Singalong Version)
   ISRC: TCAJB2411590
8. Fiddle Dee Dum (Singalong Version)
   ISRC: TCAJB2411615
9. Lah Arpeggio Scale (Singalong Version) ISRC: TCAJC2411641
10. The Aria Song (Singalong Version)
    ISRC: TCAJD2450425
11. Hullabaloo The Funky Singing Monkey (Singalong Version) ISRC: TCAJC2411682
12. Sing Hullabaloo Scale (Singalong Version)
    ISRC: TCAJB2411786
13. Buzzing Bee Butterfly (Singalong Version)
    ISRC: TCAJB2411954
14. Mademoiselle Rose Arpeggio Scale (Singalong Version) ISRC: TCAJB2412059

Hullabaloo The Funky Singing Monkey The Complete Collection: Instrumental
UPC 859798623218

1. Hullabaloo The Funky Singing Monkey (2024 Extended Version Instrumental)
   ISRC: TCAJB2448737
2. Sing Monkey Scale (Instrumental)
   ISRC: TCAGO2290435
3. Fiddle Dee Dum (Instrumental)
   ISRC: TCAGO2290446
4. Lah Arpeggio Scale (Instrumental)
   ISRC: TCAGO2290454
5. The Aria Song (Instrumental)
   ISRC: TCAGO2290463
6. Hullabaloo The Funky Singing Monkey (Instrumental) ISRC: TCAGO2290477
7. Sing Monkey Scale (Instrumental Singalong Version) ISRC: TCAJC2448698
8. Fiddle Dee Dum (Instrumental Singalong Version) ISRC: TCAJB2448711
9. Lah Arpeggio Scale (Instrumental Singalong Version) ISRC: TCAJC2448718
10. The Aria Song (Instrumental Singalong Version)
    ISRC: TCAJC2448725
11. Hullabaloo The Funky Singing Monkey (Instrumental Singalong Version) ISRC: TCAJC2448731
12. Sing Hullabaloo Scale (Instrumental Singalong Version) ISRC: TCAJC2448747
13. Buzzing Bee Butterfly (Instrumental Singalong Version) ISRC: TCAJB2448758
14. Mademoiselle Rose Arpeggio Scale (Instrumental Singalong Version) ISRC: TCAJC2448769

HULLABALOO®

® | The Hullabaloo licenced Trademark
of Nancy D'Agostino

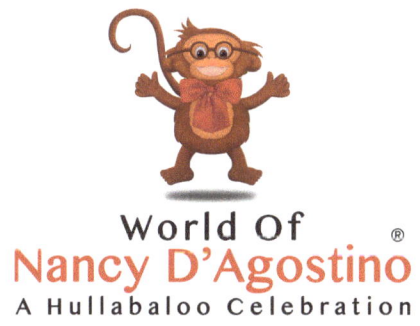 

◀ **SCAN ME**
Join in all the fun and watch out for more exciting updates!
www.worldofnancydagostino.com

◀ **SCAN ME**
There's never been a better time to learn how to sing.
www.instituteofsinging.com

The album '**Hullabaloo The Funky Singing Monkey** The Complete Collection' is also available with all the scales and songs featured in this SongBook with demonstrations by Nancy D'Agostino to guide you, followed by the instrumental music for you to practice your solo to. Then as you progress you may also want to try the '**Hullabaloo The Funky Singing Monkey** The Complete Collection: Instrumental' album and use it as an unaccompanied vocal warm-up. Available on iTunes and everywhere.

www.ingramcontent.com/pod-product-compliance
Lightning Source LLC
Chambersburg PA
CBHW041104070526
44583CB00002B/48